⊙ Collins Care for your

Cat

RSPCA
PET GUIDE

Contents

New 3rd Edition
First published in 2005 by
Collins, an imprint of
HarperCollins*Publishers*
77-85 Fulham Palace Road
Hammersmith
London W6 8JB

The Collins website is www.collins.co.uk

Collins is a registered trademark of HarperCollins Publishers Limited

10 09 08 07 06
20 19 18 17 16 15

First published as *Care for your Cat* in 1980 by
William Collins Sons & Co Ltd, London

Second edition published in 1990

Reprinted in 1991 by
HarperCollins*Publishers*
and subsequently reprinted 12 times

© Royal Society for the Prevention of Cruelty to Animals 1981, 1990, 2005
The RSPCA is a registered charity (no. 219099)
The RSPCA website is www.rspca.org.uk

Designed by: SP Creative Design
Editor: Heather Thomas
Design: Rolando Ugolini

A catalogue record for this book is available from the British Library

ISBN-13 978 0 00 719356 1
ISBN-10 0 00 719356 4

Colour reproduction by Colourscan
Printed and bound by Printing Express, Hong Kong

Foreword

Owning a cat is great fun but a huge responsibility. All animals need a regular routine and lots of love and attention. But most importantly, pets need owners who are going to stay interested in them and committed to them all their lives.

Anyone who has ever enjoyed the company of a pet knows just how strong the bond can be. Children learn the meaning of loyalty, unselfishness and friendship by growing up with animals. Elderly or lonely people often depend on a pet for company and it has been proved that animals can help in the prevention of and recovery from physical or mental illness.

The decision to bring a pet into your home should always be discussed and agreed by everyone in the family. Bear in mind that parents are ultimately responsible for the health and well-being of the animal for the whole of its lifetime. If you are not prepared for the inevitable expense, time, patience and occasional frustration involved, then the RSPCA would much rather that you didn't have a pet.

Being responsible for a pet will completely change your life but if you make the decision to go ahead, think about offering a home to one of the thousands of animals in RSPCA animal centres throughout England and Wales. There are no animals more deserving of loving owners.

As for the care of your pet, this book should provide you with all the information you need to know to keep it happy and healthy for many years to come. Enjoy the experience!

Steve Cheetham MA, VetMB, MRCVS
Chief Veterinary Officer, RSPCA

Introduction

Cats were first domesticated about 4,000 years ago by the Egyptians, and it is known from ancient works of art that have survived from those times that the Abyssinian, with its agouti coat, most resembles the cats of Ancient Egypt.

Cats were not domesticated in Europe before Roman times. In Europe, the Tabbies are thought to have been early mutations, and tabby markings still show on the kittens of the many later breeds that are descended from them.

Today there are about 100 varieties of pedigree cat to choose from, but by far the greatest number of household cats are mongrel. The breeding propensity of the cat, together with its independent lifestyle, makes a very high percentage of mongrel kittens inevitable.

Cats are perhaps the easiest of all the household pets to own, and yet because they are independent, mostly undemanding, largely self-sufficient and good survivors, some owners tend to be more casual and irresponsible about them than any other animal.

The cat is not a good choice of pet for people who are out at work all day; nor is it a good choice for a family living in a house where the cat has easy access to a busy road. You should also recognize that it is irresponsible to allow your cat to mix with others without first having been neutered.

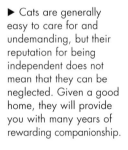

▶ Cats are generally easy to care for and undemanding, but their reputation for being independent does not mean that they can be neglected. Given a good home, they will provide you with many years of rewarding companionship.

Pedigree or mongrel?

Mongrel cats

Most household cats are mongrel, and very often they have been adopted by a family on impulse. Such easily acquired cats may not have been inoculated against the infectious cat diseases, or may not have been wormed. As soon as you acquire one, you should take it to your veterinary surgeon to be examined, and then neutered. It should be understood that although they may cost nothing at all to adopt, once taken into your household they will cost just as much as any other cat.

There is no reason, however, why these mongrel cats should not make delightful companions for us. Many of them are beautiful; all are graceful; and most are affectionate and very easy to care for. Their hardiness depends largely on their background. In general, mongrels are stronger than highly-bred animals of the same species, but if, as often happens with cats, the mongrels are the product of a mating between immature parents, then they and their kittens may be undersized and frailer than most other cats.

▲ Mongrel cats are often hardier and just as appealing as pedigrees.

Pedigree cats

Pedigree cats are usually acquired deliberately, rather than accidentally, and tend to be more carefully supervised than most mongrels. They are perhaps more prone to suffer from over-feeding and lack of exercise.

Their character is an important consideration. The Foreign and Oriental breeds, particularly the Siamese, are untypical of cats in that they are loyal to one person, from whom they demand a great deal of attention in the most vocal way. Some are notorious for being very noisy cats, especially the females when calling, but their undoubted grace and intelligence outweighs this disadvantage for most people. Orientals are also unusual in so far as they will allow themselves to be exercised on a lead.

Longhaired cats, whether pedigree or mongrel, are demanding in that they should be groomed at least once every day. In fact, devotees of longhaired breeds often groom them two or three times a day.

▲ Black British

Male or female?

If pet cats are neutered, then there is little to choose between the sexes; whether they are males or females, they will make excellent pets.

Entire males

An entire male, or tom cat, is usually regarded as unsuitable for most households, as he will spend most of his days searching out female cats on heat, returning home only to sleep and eat. Although a tom may have a pleasing and loving disposition towards people, he will frequently spray his pungent urine in the house to mark out his territory. Some toms will also leave piles of uncovered faeces in the house, as territory markers. Because they spend so much time away from home, they become involved in fights with neighbouring toms over territory or the possession of a female. Such cats soon develop a disagreeable tom-cat smell. Because they fight they are also commonly infected with FIV, the feline equavalent of AIDS (see page 35). Bites and scratches sustained during their scuffles usually become infected and may result in the formation of large abscesses, needing veterinary treatment.

Unspayed females

Unspayed females, or queens, are considered more suitable as pets, but they are difficult to contain when in season, very tiresome when they call, and likely to produce many litters in their lifetime. For these reasons, the RSPCA recommends that all household cats be neutered.

▶ To avoid the risk of unplanned pregnancies and unwanted kittens, however cute, you should be responsible as an owner and make sure you get your cat neutered.

Neutering

Why should I have my cat neutered?

The antisocial habits of an unneutered tom cat have already been described (opposite). A female cat will come into season about once every two to three weeks for around eight months of the year. As time goes on, it will become increasingly difficult to prevent her from becoming pregnant – and just as difficult to find a first-class home for every kitten (a cat can have three pregnancies a year and may have up to five or six kittens in each litter). Many thousands of unwanted kittens are destroyed each year and the least we can do as responsible owners is not to add to their number.

What does the neutering operation consist of?

In the female cat, 'spaying' consists of removing the womb and ovaries in an operation that is known as an ovarohysterectomy. In the male cat, the testicles are removed in an operation that is known as castration. Spaying and castration are both carried out by your veterinary surgeon under general anaesthesia, so the cat feels no pain. Recovery is rapid.

Should I let my cat have one litter first?

It is a popular myth that cats and dogs 'ought' to be allowed at least one litter during their lifetime. However, there is no good reason for letting your cat have a litter before you get her spayed.

Will neutering change my cat's personality?

In the female cat, there is virtually no change in personality at all. In the male, the change is only for the better – he will not wander or spray the house; he will not smell and he will not be aggressive to other cats.

Will it make my cat fat?

Neutered cats only become fat if they are overfed (see page 20). Some display symptoms caused by slight disturbances in their hormone levels. Any form of skin condition, such as eczema, may be suspected as hormonal in origin. You should seek veterinary advice in these instances so that any imbalance can be treated.

Can the operation be carried out on an older cat?

Ideally, a tom should be castrated between five and six months old, and a queen spayed from about the age of three months, but neutering can be carried out at virtually any age, provided that the cat is fit and healthy.

Breed varieties

Longhairs

The first longhaired cats were brought to Europe in the sixteenth century and were called Angoras after the city of that name (now Ankara, the capital of modern Turkey, from where they are believed to have originated). Other long-coated cats arrived from Persia

▲ Balinese

and it is from these two types that the modern Persian or Longhair breeds are descended.

The Persian has a round broad head, stubby nose, large round eyes, and tiny tufted ears. Its body is quite chunky, and its thick short legs have large round paws. Each variety is named after its coat colour, so a white-coated cat is known as the White Persian or Longhaired White, and so on. A very wide range of colours and patterns is permitted.

The original Turkish Angora still exists as a separate breed and it is also found in a wide range of colours. It has a silkier coat than the Persian and a lithe, more graceful body. It is comparatively little known. Another cat that is native to Turkey is an oddity: the Turkish Van, named after Lake Van. Unlike most cats, it enjoys swimming and playing with water. It is always white with patches of auburn or cream on the head and tail.

▲ Red Shaded Cameo Persian

▲ Longhaired Tortoiseshell and White

▶ These Red and Blue Persians look fluffy and cute but they will take a lot of your attention and time as they need daily regular grooming.

◄ The Birman was bred by Buddhist monks in Burma and worshipped as a deity. It is a sociable cat with a gentle nature.

Other longhaired breeds are more like the Angoras than the Persians in their shape, having longer noses; larger ears; longer, finer bodies; and less fullness to their coat. There are also some Longhairs that are variations on shorthaired breeds: for instance, the Balinese is the long-coated version of the popular Siamese, whereas the Somali is a longhaired Abyssinian, and the Cymric a longhaired Manx.

There are also some longhaired varieties that come from North America, among them the large Maine Coon and the unusual Ragdoll, which derives its name from its curious habit of going completely limp when it is picked up. Before committing yourself to a longhaired cat, you must remember that it will need regular daily grooming.

Shorthairs

The British Shorthair, like the Persian, is stocky with a broad round head, large round eyes, small round ears and a short thick tail. There is also the Exotic Shorthair, the true short-coated version of the Persian, which is bred from both Persian and British Shorthair parentage.

◄ The British Shorthair has a distinctive cobby body and a broad chest. This easy-going cat will be a good companion.

▶ The Abyssinian closely resembles a small wild cat. Undemanding and gentle, it likes playing games and craves its owner's attention.

The Isle of Man is not unique in being the home to a breed of tailless cat, but the Manx has a long tradition and it was once considered a lucky symbol. Another cat in which natural mutation has produced an unusual physical anomaly is the Scottish Fold, which is distinguished by its folded ears. The other shorthaired breeds have a quite different body configuration from that of the British and Exotic Shorthairs, and these are described collectively as Foreign Shorthairs.

Cats of the Foreign group tend to be slim and lithe, with long faces, large ears, long slim legs and long pointed tails. The Abyssinian is said to resemble the cats that were revered in Ancient Egypt and, uniquely among cats, it has a 'ticked' coat. The Russian Blue has a distinctive dense coat, which is dark slate grey in colour, and green eyes, whereas the similarly coloured Korat, from Thailand, has a smooth coat and a heart-shaped face. Burmese cats tend to be slightly stockier and they are renowned for their intelligence and good nature.

▼ The Korat is an ancient breed which originated in Thailand. Its head is heart-shaped and it has luminous green eyes.

Other Foreign Shorthairs include the shiny black Bombay, Burmillas and the distinctive Rexes. There are two main breeds of curly-coated Rex cats, which are named after the English counties in which they were first discovered: the Cornish Rex and the Devon Rex. The Cornish has the more luxurious coat and is quite Oriental in configuration, while the Devon, with its softly-waved coat, has a rather pixie-like look.

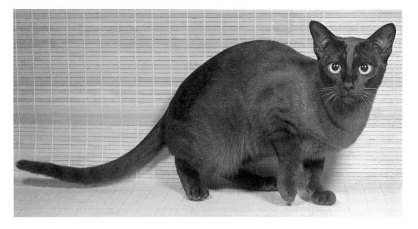

◄ The Burmese is playful and confident and, unlike many cats, enjoys being sociable with its owners. Demanding and attention seeking, it hates being left alone and thus is not a suitable pet for people who work away from home.

Orientals

Siamese and the varieties that are derived from them are known as Oriental cats. All these cats are slim with very distinctive wedge-shaped heads, large pointed ears, long slim legs and tiny oval paws. They are both inquisitive and intelligent. The Siamese have colour only on the 'points' of their mask (face), ears, legs, paws and tail. They are named after the colour of the points. Thus the seal brown is known as the Seal Point Siamese, and so on. All Siamese cats (and one of the derived breeds, the Oriental or Foreign White), have brilliant blue eyes, whereas all the other Oriental Shorthairs have bright green eyes and, having lost the gene that restricts their coat colour to the points, are evenly coloured all over.

▼ The Siamese is vocal, intelligent and demanding. It craves human company and is very boisterous. You should own one only if you are prepared to play with it every day.

Biology

Backbone The combination of an extremely supple backbone and powerful back muscles gives the cat a great range of movement, including the ability to arch its back in this way. It also allows a falling cat to twist in mid-air to right its position for a safe landing.

Tail The magnificent tail of the cat has many biological uses. It is a muffler against the cold; a balance in climbing and jumping; a protection against flies; a communications signal; and both a warning and a distraction to an enemy. The curious tailless Manx cat has not fallen victim to the practice of tail-docking – it is a mutant form of cat with only three tail vertebrae. Other cats may have as many as 24 vertebrae.

Claws A cat's claws are of great importance, being both a weapon of attack and defence, and an aid to climbing. Cats take care to keep their claws in good trim, sharpening them on a scratching post by pulling off the damaged outer layer of claw to expose a new layer beneath. When they are not in use, all but the dew claws are retracted into a protective sheath which saves them from becoming blunted.

Eyes The cat hunts more by sight than smell, aided by extremely efficient eyesight which adjusts instantaneously to changing lighting conditions. In bright light the pupil will contract to a mere longitudinal slit; in poor light it will dilate to take advantage of the faintest gleam. In very bad light the cat's eyes appear to shine, giving rise to the claim that cats can see in the dark. This is not so, but in poor lighting the eyes, like the road studs named after them, are able to reflect back any available light so that they appear to glow.

Whiskers The whiskers, or vibrissae, are modified hairs which serve as tactile organs. Whiskers are extremely sensitive to touch, since they grow from hair follicles that are abundantly well supplied with nerve-endings. It is also thought that they allow a cat to judge the width of an opening, since the extent of the whiskers, from tip to tip, is equivalent to the maximum width of the cat's body.

Ears Cats have a well-developed sense of hearing and can move the external ears (pinnae) in the direction of sound, collecting and conducting the sound waves to the eardrum for transmission to the inner ear. The pinnae also allow the cat to judge the distance and direction of sound. A sound from a particular source is heard slightly differently in each ear, and from this the cat can estimate its source accurately. The inner ear is the organ of balance. When its fluid-filled cavities and canals are stimulated by tilting and rotating movements, reflex actions are triggered returning the body to its normal position. This is important to an agile animal like the cat, and because of it the cat is reputed always to land on its feet.

Tongue The surface of the cat's tongue is covered with small projections, or papillae, that account for its characteristic roughness. This surface makes the tongue an effective tool for feeding, particularly for rasping flesh from bones, and an equally effective tool for grooming.

Teeth Being a naturally short-faced animal, the cat has a set of only 30 teeth, whereas a dog has 42. An adult cat has 12 incisors, 4 canines, 10 premolars and 4 molars. The cat's teeth are those of the true carnivore, perfectly adapted for the diet of a meat-eater. The prominent canines, or fangs, are used to kill prey and to tear meat from a carcass. The molars, or cheek teeth, have blade-like edges for slicing flesh into pieces small enough to swallow.

Selecting a cat

Once you have decided that you want to share your life with a cat, you have to make up your mind whether you would prefer a pedigree or a mongrel, a male or a female, an adult cat or a kitten.

Kittens

These are endearing and full of fun, and few people can resist them. However, they do need your care and attention – house training and feeding up to five times a day to begin with – and can be very time-consuming during the first few months. They will also enthusiastically claw curtains and chair legs, and if there are young children or elderly people about, they are in danger of being trodden underfoot or causing an accident. Although they soon grow from playful balls of destruction into amiable and often perfect pets, for these reasons many people prefer to consider taking on an adult cat rather than a young kitten.

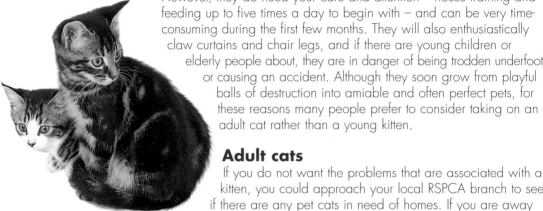

▲ When choosing a kitten, make sure you see it with its mother and the rest of the litter; this will give you a good idea of its health and temperament.

Adult cats

If you do not want the problems that are associated with a kitten, you could approach your local RSPCA branch to see if there are any pet cats in need of homes. If you are away from home for most of the day, then you might decide to get two cats, so they are company for one another. Rather than acquiring a cat on impulse, decide exactly what you would like, then set about finding the right pet for you.

Is a cat the right pet for you?

Before you get a cat or kitten, ask yourself a few basic questions.
- Do you have a garden or safe access to the great outdoors?
- Are you home for at least part of the day, every day?
- Are you willing to put up with possible claw damage to furnishings?
- Are you willing to pay for vaccinations and veterinary treatment? Pet insurance can help to cover some of these costs. All but those cats that are kept specifically for breeding should be neutered before six months of age, and all kittens and young cats should be vaccinated against Feline Infectious Enteritis, Feline Leukaemia Virus and Feline Influenza, which require booster vaccinations throughout their lifetime.
- Are you willing to pay for boarding your cat when you go on holiday, or do you have caring neighbours who will feed and look after it for you?

If you cannot honestly answer 'yes' to all these questions, then you should think very carefully before you acquire either an adult cat or a kitten.

Sources

Ask your friends, neighbours and local vets, and check the local newspaper advertisements rather than pet shops. The regional RSPCA or cat rescue office may also be able to help you to find a suitable cat. Many people cannot keep their pets for a variety of reasons and are happy to find a good home for their adult cat. You should also enquire about vaccinations and find out as much as you possibly can about the cat's background. Knowing its habits and fears will help to settle it in and make it feel at home.

Sometimes a cat might 'adopt' you, turning up daily on your doorstep. If this should happen, you must take care that you are not inadvertently enticing it away from its home with your attentions.

If you want to find out more about pedigree cats, you should first read up about them in an up-to-date reference book. Visit a cat show where you will be able to see many types of pedigree cats, and where you can meet and talk with their owners and breeders.

The important thing is to choose a cat that will suit you and your lifestyle. Cats do vary greatly, and it is vital that you have the time to care for your pet and you are both of the same basic temperament.

▲ Whether you choose a pedigree or a mongrel, a cat can make the ideal pet and companion. Many cats live happily together and it is perfectly possible to introduce a new cat into an already established feline household.

◄ Pedigree cats, like this Birman Sealpoint, can be quite expensive to buy, but they come with the reassurance of a reliable source and also a well documented background.

Housing

Cat bed

The only accommodation that a cat really needs is a good bed, which may be any comfortable chair, box or basket, but should not be one of the household's beds or chairs. Fleas sometimes cling to even the best-kept cats and will lay their eggs in bedding or upholstery. A variety of manufactured cat beds is available, made of fibreglass, rigid plastic, canvas or basketwork. Beds should be raised off the ground, clear of draughts and dampness, and when a bed has no legs, the base must be slightly domed to leave some air space underneath.

A washable cushion or blanket will keep the cat comfortable, and provided that it always has access to its bed, heating is unnecessary, except rarely in the case of elderly or sick cats, or for very young kittens in severe weather conditions.

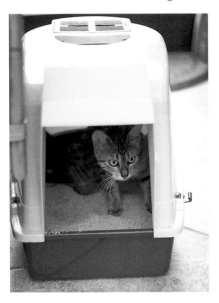

▲ Hooded litter trays can offer an extra degree of privacy, especially for nervous animals, but they are not ideal for all cats.

Litter tray

Cats are the most fastidious of all animals, and from a very early age, they will scratch out a hole before they defecate and then cover over the traces with earth. This has a natural survival value in the wild, as it serves to hide the presence of the nest of young kittens, and in captivity makes the cat one of the cleanest pets to own.

Cats can be easily house trained to urinate and defecate in a litter tray, which is filled with dry earth, sand, or a proprietary cat litter. The tray will need to be kept scrupulously clean, and in a secluded position where the cat will feel that it is private enough to use. Hooded litter trays are ideal for those cats that prefer their toilet arrangements to be private. The hood lifts off for ease of cleaning, and the extra-deep base prevents the litter from being scratched out on to the floor. City cats, with no safe access to a garden, may need to use a tray for life, and many adult cats will need one at night.

Scratching post

The cat uses its claws in climbing, in defence, and in attack, and it has to keep them in immaculate condition if they are to serve these purposes. They are normally held sheathed in order to protect them from being blunted in wear. Many cats will sharpen their claws on a tree trunk in the garden, whereas others will select a particular item of furniture or upholstery in the house and they may damage it severely with constant use.

In an attempt to forestall such damage, some owners provide a scratching post for their cat. Any good-sized length of log with its bark on is suitable. Alternatively, a piece of sacking or heavy upholstery material nailed to a board makes a satisfactory decoy from armchairs.

A wide range of manufactured scratching posts is available in most pet accessory stores. These include items such as a bark-covered post which is impregnated with catnip; another, covered with textured cardboard; and a carpet or rope-covered post on its own stand.

Cat door

It is important that pet cats should have access to the house at all times during the day and night. If they are unable to get into their own home and bed whenever they want, cats are likely to wander off for long periods, getting involved in fights with other cats, and are at great risk of being injured by traffic, or even stolen. However, eventually these unwanted cats may decide to seek another home elsewhere with a more friendly family.

A cat door can be fitted easily into an external door of your house and is extremely useful. It will provide your cat with an easy means of access to the house. Cat doors are manufactured in such a way that they are burglar-proof if fitted correctly. They measure about 15 cm (6 in) square and should be fixed out of reach of security locks and bolts.

Some cat doors can be opened by the cat by means of a radio-controlled device fitted to a safety collar. These cat doors are ideal (if your cat does not object to wearing the collar) for use in areas where stray cats may decide to check out your cat's home for food.

Some models have two-way flaps, whereas with others the cat needs to lift the flap to return through the door. Many can be adjusted so that your cat can come into the house but not go out again.

The RSPCA recommends that all cats are microchipped.

▼ As soon as your cat has learnt to use the cat flap, it will have the opportunity to control its own environment.

Settling in

Although it is a fairly simple matter to introduce a young kitten to its new home and to a new family and pets, it is more difficult with an adult cat. Cats are such creatures of habit that they do not take kindly to any change of home or routine. Because of this, it is necessary to make proper preparations before introducing a cat to your house.

Getting ready for your cat

First, decide where you will keep the cat until it has made friends with you, your family and other pets, if you have them. Make sure that the room or area is escape-proof and that there are no spaces into which the cat may crawl to hide, and possibly get trapped. Cats can and do squeeze into remarkably small holes – the back of a boiler for instance – and many cats have hidden in chimneys. Provide the new cat with a litter tray and a set of food and water bowls. Make sure that the bed you select is cosy and warm and that the cat will feel secure in it amidst the strange surroundings of its new home. If possible, bring some of the cat's bedding from the animal centre or its old home.

Pheromones

Cats use pheromones to signal their moods, such as fear or calmness. These substances are now made as diffusers which can plug into a mains socket.

◄ Many cats enjoy their owner's company and can be rewarding companions while retaining a high degree of legendary independence.

These products will help your new cat to settle in to its new home. Ask your veterinary surgeon for advice on them and which ones to choose.

Getting to know your cat

Make a great fuss of your new pet, constantly using its name, and it will soon show its acceptance of you by scent marking you, rubbing its forehead and lips against your hands and legs. When this happens, and you are confident that the cat will come to you, you may make your first excursions to other parts of the house, and eventually into the garden.

Children must be taught to handle the cat correctly and to treat it with respect at all times. Resident pets may not immediately accept a new cat into the home, and great care must be exercised while the newcomer is being introduced. Resident pets must not be made to feel jealous and the new addition must not feel threatened or intimidated. If you can borrow a kitten pen, the new cat may be popped in this while your other pets are first introduced, to guard against possible fights.

▲ A wire mesh door will afford a cat a good view of its surroundings, something many cats will appreciate. When you bring your cat (or cats) home, open the door of the pet carrier and give them time to come out and explore their new surroundings.

Feeding

Cats are by nature predatory animals, catching mice, young rats, birds and, sometimes, fish and amphibians with great stealth and skill. Their method is to lie in wait for their victim, or to stalk it up to the moment of the final pounce. The shortness of their muzzles makes it difficult for cats to reach out and snap at their prey with their jaws. Instead their style is to bring down the prey with their paws, and deliver the death blow with their teeth. This makes it appear as though the cat is playing with its prey.

Hunting ability is, to some extent, a matter of heredity, some cats being notoriously better and more skilful than others. Cats that are well fed and in peak condition are likely to be better hunters than others, and only cats in prime condition are able to tackle a rat. This hunting instinct cannot be erased from the cat's nature, but bird-lovers should avoid enticing birds into a cat's territory with food, nest boxes and so on.

Feeding suggestions

An adult cat will need about 50 kilocalories per 450 g (1 lb) of body weight per day. A sedentary neutered cat may keep fit on a little less; a very active cat may require a little more; and a lactating female's requirement may be as high as 125–150 kilocalories per 450 g (1 lb) of her body weight while feeding an average litter of four kittens.

Most cats seem to thrive best on two regular daily meals, but old cats may need smaller meals at more frequent intervals, rather like young kittens. In some cases, old cats with kidney disease or constipation may require special diets and veterinary advice should be sought. There may be a tendency for neutered animals to put on excess weight with age, but this should be controlled with a little adjustment to their diet. You should cut

A feeding guide

Age	Average body weight kg (lb)	Daily food requirements g (oz)	Number of meals per day
5 months	2 kg (4½ lb)	170 g (6 oz)	3
7–8 months	3 kg (6½ lb)	200 g (7 oz)	2–3
Adult	4–4.5 kg (9–10 lb)	185–225 g (6½–8 oz)	1–2
Pregnant female	3.5 kg (7½ lb)	250 g (8½ oz)	2–3
Lactating female	2.5 kg (5½ lb)	400 g (14 oz)	4

out all cereals and feed good quality, high-protein, low-fat meals in small quantities. Your cat's general appearance will tell you whether or not you are feeding it correctly. An obese cat is obviously having too much food, while a thin cat is either having too little food or is suffering from internal parasites or a disease. The signs that a cat's diet is lacking in certain nutrients include a dry, scurfy coat, a warm, dry nose, dull eyes, flaking claws, offensive-smelling faeces and bad breath.

Nutritional requirements for a healthy cat

For your cat to be really fit and healthy, you should ensure that it is fed a balanced diet that contains all the essential nutrients it needs.

Protein

At least 25 per cent of an adult cat's diet should consist of protein; 35–40 per cent if it is a breeding pedigree. Protein is found in muscle meat, fish, eggs and cheese. Cats must have some protein of animal origin. Unlike humans and, with care, dogs, they cannot maintain good health on a vegetarian diet. Cats that cannot digest milk may be able to cope with plain yoghurt.

Fats

Cats can digest a high proportion of fats in their diet; up to 25 per cent fat is recommended by feline nutritionists for young, growing cats. Fats provide concentrated forms of energy and contain fatty acids which promote healthy skin and coats. Fats also contain fat-soluble vitamins A, D, E and K. Fats are present in some meat, butter and cooking oils.

Carbohydrates

Cooked grains and pulses are sometimes fed to cats in order to bulk out a protein-rich diet, but they are not necessary for a cat's well-being.

Vitamins and minerals

Cats that are fed a varied, well-balanced diet will obtain all the valuable vitamins and minerals they require. Vitamin/mineral supplements should not be given to your cat without seeking veterinary advice first.

● **Vitamin A** A cat's requirement for this vitamin can be supplied by feeding a good general diet and adding 28 g (1 oz) of lightly cooked liver one day a week. Too much vitamin A can be dangerous, leading to the laying down of excess bone in the spine and joints.

▼ As a really responsible owner, you should ensure that you offer your cat a balanced, healthy diet.

● **Vitamin B group** The B vitamins may be destroyed by cooking and therefore you should always select canned cat foods in which these essential vitamins have been replaced in processing.

● **Vitamin C** This is generally considered unnecessary for cats except when recovering from illness or having antibiotic treatment. It can be administered in the form of the orange-flavoured syrup sold for human babies.

● **Vitamins D and E** The cat's needs for these are low compared to those of the dog or human, and they are provided in a normal diet.

Fresh food

A butcher or fishmonger will supply good but inexpensive fresh meat and fish which are suitable for feeding raw, and offal which must be cooked. Always feed a variety of food for the best nutritional balance, and remember that cheap meat is as good, nutritionally, as expensive meat. Avoid bones that may splinter or lodge in the throat.

Cats take a little vegetable matter directly in the wild, and some indirectly by eating the stomach contents of their prey. In captivity, very small amounts of vegetables or cereal, such as wholemeal bread, may be added to their diet as a source of roughage.

Convenience foods

More expensive but ready-prepared meals are available as canned or packeted cat food. These should always be fed exactly according to the manufacturer's instructions. Dehydrated cat foods must always be accompanied by large quantities of drinking water. Without this, a cat may sometimes develop a urinary tract infection.

Drinking water and milk

Many cats prefer to drink from a dripping tap or puddle, rather than from their own water bowl, but fresh drinking water must nevertheless be provided. Chemical-tasting tap water can be made more palatable by leaving it to stand for a while or by the use of a commercial water filter. In some cats, milk can cause severe diarrhoea, so routine feeding is not recommended.

◀ You should make sure that your cat always has plenty of fresh drinking water available.

Grooming

Shorthaired cats
The cat's own tongue is a well-adapted tool for grooming its natural, i.e. shorthaired, coat. Strictly speaking, there is no need for owners to groom shorthaired cats for most of the year, although brushing does keep the cat tractable and allows close examination of its condition.

Moulting and hair balls
Cats normally moult twice a year, but moulting is frequently prolonged by poor feeding or by ill-health. When a shorthaired cat is moulting, its owner's attention is vital. During moulting, an ungroomed cat will swallow some loose hairs, some of which may become lodged in the digestive tract and become matted with food to form hard balls. These hair balls can cause serious blockages, and they may even need veterinary attention. Grooming will help to prevent them.

If cats swallow hair, they will eat grass as an emetic to make themselves vomit. For this reason, grass should always be available to them. City cats may need to have some grown in a flower pot.

▲ This Siamese cat is demonstrating the use of its tongue as a most effective grooming tool.

Grooming shorthairs
Most shorthaired cats will benefit greatly from regular grooming – not only when they are moulting – so you should get your cat accustomed to being groomed from an early age. Use a very fine-toothed comb to effectively remove loose and dead hair from the cat's coat along with dead flakes of skin, and fleas, too, if they are are present. The comb will catch fleas and will also remove the tell-tale dark flecks of their excreta from the coat.

▶ Grooming itself is a natural behaviour for a cat. However, excessive grooming can lead to the development of hair balls in the cat's stomach.

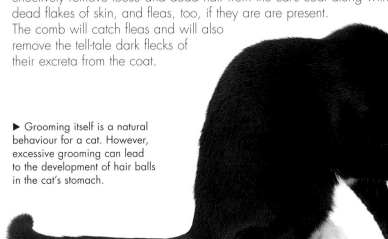

Longhaired cats

Longhaired cats are quite unable to groom themselves adequately. Their long fur is the result of breeding from longhaired mutants which would probably have died out in the wild. No wild cat has hair of this length; and no cat is capable of grooming its fur by itself without your help. Unless they are groomed daily, longhaired cats may develop a seriously matted coat.

Daily grooming

This is absolutely essential for all the longhaired breeds, and many experienced fanciers recommend two or even three grooming sessions a day. Any burr, small twig or fragment of a dead leaf will otherwise quickly become the centre of a tangle that will have to be cut out. In really extreme cases, the badly matted longhaired cat may need to be anaesthetized by a veterinary surgeon for de-matting.

From a very early age, all longhaired cats will need to become accustomed to their coat being brushed out and combed every day as a matter of routine. At first, you must take care not to overtax a kitten's patience. In time, it will get accustomed to the experience and may even come to enjoy it. For your part, it will help you to bond with your cat.

Bathing a cat

This is not necessary, although some white cats like bathing, notably the Turkish Van. Dry shampoos are available for occasional use.

▲ Grass is used as an emetic. City cats with no access to a grassy area will need turf or grass grown in a flower pot. Longhairs are particularly prone to hair balls.

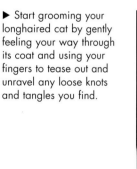

▶ Start grooming your longhaired cat by gently feeling your way through its coat and using your fingers to tease out and unravel any loose knots and tangles you find.

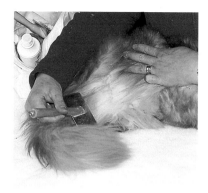

▲ Brush or comb the fur away from the cat's head towards the tail.

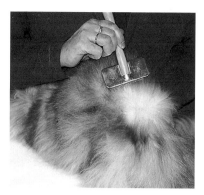

▲ Comb or brush the fur in the opposite direction, without dragging it.

▲ Gently brush the ruff of fur around the cat's neck and head.

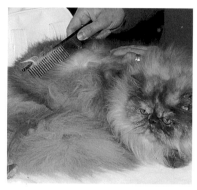

▲ Carefully comb or cut out any knots and tangles that remain.

▲ Brush the fur underneath, teasing out any knots with your fingers or a comb.

▲ Check the cat's ears, nose and eyes, gently wiping away any mucus.

Handling and training

When lifting a cat, always place one hand beneath the chest and the other around the hind legs so that the entire weight is supported. If the cat is immediately turned towards the handler it will be able to cling on to his or her clothing for extra security. Do not pick up your cat by the scruff of the neck, as this is too great a strain on all but very young kittens. Similarly, it is wrong to pick up your cat by the front quarters only, allowing the hind legs to hang down.

Cats should be accustomed to being handled correctly from an early age, and also to having all the parts of their body touched, whether or not this is at grooming time. It is a good idea to institute a regular routine for checking the cat's coat behind the ears and along the spine for signs of fleas (see page 38); gently cleaning inside the ear-flaps, and extending the claws to check for injuries. Children must always be taught to respect the cat, and to handle it gently and safely.

Emergency handling

It may be impossible to handle a cat normally in an emergency, for instance after a road accident, because it will scratch out in terror at anyone who goes near it. The safest method is to drop a blanket on to the cat and wrap it round firmly with just the head free. In this way, it can be transported safely to a veterinary surgeon for treatment.

When rescuing a trapped cat, it would be wise to wear strong gloves to protect your hands, and as soon as possible take hold of the cat's front paws to prevent them scratching your face. Holding a cat by the scruff of the neck will help to prevent you from being bitten.

Training your cat

It is important to choose a simple, effective name for your cat and to make sure that it identifies with its name by constant use, particularly at feeding and petting times. Never use the cat's name in a cross way. Scolding is best done by sharp clapping of the hands when the cat is caught in the act of misbehaving, and rewards for good behaviour can consist of cat 'treats' or titbits, or stroking in the cat's favourite way.

It is essential that both scolding and rewards are given at the time of the behaviour needing correction or fixing, otherwise the cat will be unable to connect your behavioural response with its own.

Cats are very sensitive creatures and will never forgive or forget being smacked by their owner. They do not like being shouted at either, but you might find a low, growling 'no' works well when your cat is seen to be doing something unacceptable. You may also lightly grasp the loose skin at the scruff of the neck and give the cat a little shake, rather as a mother cat does to its kittens.

On the whole, cats will accept very basic 'training' but they may or may not do as you want, when you want it. The sooner that training is started, the more effective it is likely to be.

◄ Cats soon learn to recognize their owner's voice and to respond.

Exercise

▶ Given a garden in which to roam freely, a cat will soon discover its favourite vantage point from which to survey its territory from up above.

It is a characteristic of the entire cat family that while they are capable of short bursts of energy, they do not possess a dog's stamina for more sustained exercise. In many ways, this makes them particularly suitable as household pets because they are content to spend a great deal of their time just sleeping and resting.

So far as possible, all cats should be encouraged to stay close to their own house and garden, which can be achieved with those cats that have been neutered. Tom cats that have been castrated will have less desire to roam than entire cats, and, similarly, those females that have been spayed will not be so restless, and nor will they entice the local toms to come visiting their house with their calling.

Even if the family cat is not free to exercise at will, it is obvious that any cat should have the freedom to play in its own garden every day. The cat will be most content if the garden is rather wild, with trees for it to climb and bushes to stalk through. In particular, cats like a high vantage point from which to survey their territory, and they will often climb up trees or on to a rooftop to secure one. Although a cat will find its way through any fence or over any wall, neutered cats will usually stay within 'their' territory.

Collars and leads

It is even possible to exercise some breeds of cat on a lead. Many of the Oriental breeds, and in particular the Siamese, will wear a cat collar comfortably and will allow themselves to be led by their owner.

It might seem that a cat collar, when used with a name disc, is an excellent way of identifying a cat in the case of a mishap, but this is not always so. The only really satisfactory design is the type where the

▶ Some Oriental cats, such as this regal Burmese, will quite happily wear a harness and can even be trained to walk on a lead.

buckle snaps apart when pushed hard. A cat that is trapped in a tree by its own collar is bound to struggle and may well twist the collar into a figure-of-eight shape until it becomes a noose.

Indoor games

Although it is not desirable, it is possible to keep a cat indoors. Cats kept entirely in the house must be given lots of play and exercise opportunities, otherwise they soon become lazy, lethargic and possibly overweight. You should set aside a period for playtime each day and encourage your cat to chase after a feather on a string, ping-pong balls or cat toys that are suitable for tossing around the room. Some cats become adept at retrieving, and you will tire of the game long before your feline friend. Large cardboard boxes can be stuck together with non-toxic glue and have interconnecting holes cut through to form a maze. Cats love leaping into boxes, hiding and pouncing out through the different holes.

▼ Always provide toys and indoor furniture or a scratching post for cats that are confined indoors.

Wooden step ladders can be converted into the ideal climbing toys for housebound cats: carpet off-cuts can be tacked or stuck to the treads and a padded cushion fixed to the topmost step. Some of the larger pet product manufacturers sell wonderful carpet-covered 'cat trees' which fit from the floor to the ceiling of the average room. Cats love to shin up the 'trunk' and use the various 'branches' for sitting or sleeping. Some of the cat trees have hollow drums at the bottom for holding a removable toilet tray or a cat's bed. There are all manner of sophisticated feline furniture and toys, which are designed expressly for confined cats, and although many of the items are expensive, they do last for many years and provide endless hours of exercise and fun for your cat.

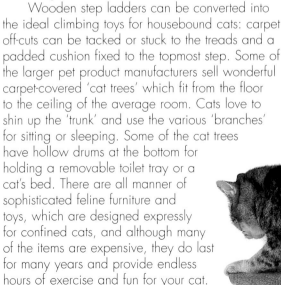

Travelling and boarding

▼ One of the best ways to make sure your cat will get reliable care when you're away on holiday is to board it at a reputable cattery. Inspect the facilities in advance and find out what the health requirements are. Be sure to book early.

Whenever you take your cat anywhere by car you should confine it within a suitable, comfortable carrier or buy an appropriate harness which can be secured to a seat belt. An unconfined cat can be a hazard when driving and may run off when the car door is opened.

To habituate your cat to its carrier, start by putting it inside at odd times. Make sure that there is a soft blanket inside the carrier and perhaps a favourite toy. It is best to carry out carrier training just before feeding time, so that the cat comes to regard the carrier as leading to good things. If you habitually make very long journeys, get a carrier or

cage large enough to contain a small litter tray and some hook-on food and water containers as well as your cat's cushion or blanket.

Cat carriers range from sturdy wooden crates designed for air travel to fold-out cardboard containers suitable only for emergency use. In between there are wicker baskets of several different designs, some of which convert to beds by removing the front wire grill. Plastic covered wire-mesh carriers are very secure and easily cleaned. Cats like them because they can see out and do not feel too constrained. There are also many designs made in plastic and fibreglass.

When you are away

At holiday time it may be possible to arrange for a friend, neighbour or relative to visit the house two or three times a day to tend to the cat. This is probably the best method of all, since cats prefer to remain in their own home, and although they may miss the family, at least their own surroundings are unchanged.

It is not a good idea to move the cat into somebody else's home, from which it will immediately try to escape. Neither is it feasible to leave the cat alone to hunt and find its own food. This is both cruel and illegal, and is classed as abandonment in law. The alternative is to arrange for your cat to board at a good cattery. At well-run catteries, the cats have their own cabins, which are very secure with a covered run, litter tray and an elevated sleeping section with a heater. This is approached by a ramp, and the cat enters by way of a cat door.

Any cattery will need as much notice as possible and will want to see an up-to-date vaccination certificate. No good cattery will accept cats which have not been inoculated against the major infectious diseases.

▼ A cat carrier will be essential for transporting your cat safely. Make the unit cosy and allow your cat to explore it outside of visits to the veterinary clinic in order to prevent a 'negative' association being formed.

Travelling safely

When a cat needs to be moved from the house in order to be taken to the veterinary surgeon, cattery, pet show or on holiday, it must always be secured in a box. Any strong cardboard box with a safe base will serve as a temporary carrier. Air holes must be punched in the sides and some string tied securely to form a handle. However, a determined and frightened cat will quickly escape, and therefore a purpose-made cat carrier is much better and safer. Make sure that you choose a design that can be cleaned out easily if the cat has an 'accident' from fright.

The healthy cat

Most cats are very healthy and resilient, with such quick reflexes and good agility that they survive, with their legendary 'nine lives', in situations where slower animals would perish. Getting to know your cat will help you to recognize any deterioration in its condition or change in its behaviour.

Prevention is the best cure

A cat's natural resistance to disease is lowered by cold, damp living conditions and poor food. Like humans, cats can suffer from the malfunction of certain organs, such as the heart, kidneys and liver, and the best guard against this is prevention.

To do this, you must ensure that your cat receives a good, varied diet (see page 20). A faddy eater may not be taking in sufficient nutrition to keep it in tip-top condition, and a cat that habitually drinks too little can be prone to kidney and digestive troubles later on in life.

A cat that is cooped up indoors alone all day will soon become either frustrated and destructive or bored and lazy. Lack of exercise coupled with the wrong food can lead to obesity, which, in turn, can contribute to a variety of feline health problems.

Even if a cat is accustomed to going out at night, and is too old to change the habit of a lifetime, it must always have access – perhaps by means of a cat door (see page 17) – to the dry, warm retreat of its home, particularly as the cat begins to age.

Infectious diseases

These may be transmitted in several ways: through droplets sneezed, coughed or breathed out by the infected cat, which are then breathed in by a susceptible cat, or through contaminated drink, feeding bowls or bedding. Flies, fleas or other agents, with faeces, urine, vomit, pus or saliva can pass on disease from an infected cat, or illness may be passed by direct contact between cats which live together.

Symptoms of disease

The first symptom of disease in the cat is generally loss of appetite, either partially or completely, and when this happens the caring owner will immediately look for the cause. Most cats will eagerly await their regular meals and will consume the entire contents of the dish within minutes. Some cats are more finicky, but any change in the cat's normal eating pattern should be treated as a warning sign of illness.

Other signs of the onset of an illness are indicated by changes in the cat's appearance or behaviour. It may sit hunched up or resent being touched. It may sit over its water bowl but seem unable to drink. It may go repeatedly to its toilet tray but appear to be unable to pass either urine or faeces. Its eyes may look dull, or the third eyelid may appear like a skin at the inner corners of the eyes. The cat may stop washing and its fur may become odorous. Its breath may smell foul or it might sneeze, drool, vomit or have diarrhoea. When you contact your veterinary surgeon, be sure to list all the symptoms and the order of their onset to help him or her make an accurate diagnosis.

Signs of health

Abdomen	Without wounds, growths, and sores; not distended or unduly sensitive.
Anus	This should be clean, with no staining or scouring; motions passed should be without persistent constipation or diarrhoea.
Appetite	This should be good; weight should be maintained in adults, and growth in kittens; there should be no persistent vomiting.
Breathing	Should be even and quiet, with no wheezing, coughing or excessive effort.
Claws	There should be no splits, thorns, splinters or damaged pads.
Coat	Should be well-groomed, glossy; free from parasites, their eggs and faeces, loose hairs and scurviness. No baldness or patches.
Demeanour	Watchful, even at rest; quickly responsive to sounds; quiet and contented.
Ears	These should be pricked to catch sounds; free of discharge; no irritation, scratching or shaking of head.
Eyes	Clear, not bloodshot; third eyelid not showing; no discharge or watering.
Faeces	Droppings should be buried, except sometimes by toms marking territory as dogs do. There should be no persistent constipation or diarrhoea.
Movement	Free movement, agile, with no stiffness in joints or gait. Weight should be evenly distributed.
Skin	Should be supple, with no scurf, inflammation, parasites or sores.
Teeth	Teeth should be clean, free of tartar; gums should be pink, not inflamed, white or yellowish.
Urine	This should be passed effortlessly, with no pain. It is normal for toms to spray in the house and garden to mark territory, as dogs do.

Vaccinations

▲ Regular booster vaccinations will give your pet a lifelong protection from the major illnesses that are most likely to threaten it.

Although there is a whole range of illnesses from which a cat may suffer, some of the more serious infectious cat diseases can be prevented by a programme of routine vaccinations. Extremely effective vaccines are available to protect against Feline Infectious Enteritis, Feline Leukaemia Virus (FeLV) and Feline Upper Respiratory Disease (FURD), which is more commonly known as Feline Influenza or 'cat flu'. There is also now a vaccination to prevent chlamidial infection.

When to vaccinate

Depending on the make of vaccine, injections may be started in the young kitten from eight, ten or twelve weeks, with booster doses being given on veterinary advice. It is common to have adult cats boosted at regular intervals, usually annually or once every two years. If your cat is to be boarded or, if a breeding queen, sent away for mating, it is important to have its vaccinations and boosters given in good time, as immunity may not be complete for several days after the injections.

Cats should have a certificate recording all the details of their vaccinations. If you are not sure when your cat was last immunized, ask your veterinary surgeon to begin a programme of boosters which should be continued throughout the cat's life.

Major infectious diseases

Vaccinating your cat will provide it with effective immunization against the following major infectious feline diseases.

Feline Infectious Enteritis

This is a common virus disease with symptoms of abdominal pain, vomiting and collapse. The cat suffers severe dehydration and, although it is obviously thirsty, it will not be able to drink. Once the disease is contracted, it is difficult to effect a cure and immunization is the only real safeguard. This disease spreads rapidly among cats, and kittens are especially vulnerable.

Feline Influenza

An infectious disease common in summertime, 'cat flu' is caused by a group of viruses affecting the upper respiratory tract, with symptoms of sneezing, running eyes and nose, and excessive salivation. Prompt veterinary treatment can usually cure Feline Influenza but cats frequently become carriers. This is why vaccination is essential to protect your own and other cats. Vaccination of young cats is especially important.

Feline Leukaemia

This is now known to be caused by a virus (FeLV) which is spread by saliva, urine and faeces. It is not as contagious as other common feline diseases and seems mainly to be spread by close contact over a long period of time. Vaccination of young cats is especially important.

Other infectious diseases

There are also some less common but serious infectious diseases for which no vaccine is as yet commercially available.

● Feline Immunodeficiency Virus (FIV) This disease causes an immune suppression which is similar to HIV in humans. It is transmitted by fighting and biting, and entire tom cats are often infected.

● Feline Infectious Peritonitis (FIP) This inflammation of the peritoneum or lining of the abdomen is caused by a virus. It is a serious condition for which there is at present no cure.

Ailments

Digestive problems

A cat will regulate any minor digestive disorders by eating grass to make itself sick. Occasional bouts of constipation can be relieved by a tablespoonful of medicinal paraffin or olive oil, but you should always consult your veterinary surgeon if it continues for more than a couple of days. Diarrhoea can be caused by milk or it may be a symptom of a number of more serious ailments. You could try feeding beaten egg white or a little boiled rice to the cat. Again, trouble persisting for more than a day or so should be referred to your veterinary surgeon.

Ears

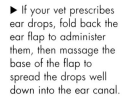

▶ If your vet prescribes ear drops, fold back the ear flap to administer them, then massage the base of the flap to spread the drops well down into the ear canal.

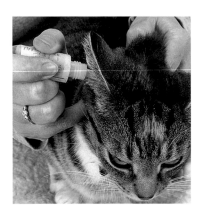

A number of irritants can cause cats to scratch persistently at their ears. These include ear mites (for which your vet can supply drops), a small seed which has worked its way into the ear, or an abscessed wound which has been inflicted by another cat. As a cat's ear is extremely delicate and vulnerable, seek help from your vet rather than attempting to solve the problem yourself.

Hair balls

Longhaired cats, if they are not meticulously groomed, will suffer from hair balls from time to time. By ingesting their own hair in the course of grooming themselves, a clot of matted hair will form in the gut. Usually a cat will solve the problem itself by chewing grass to regurgitate the hair ball, but severe cases may need an operation.

Skin complaints

▲ When a cat is seen eating some grass, it is probably attempting to remove a hair ball from its stomach.

If small spots or sore patches appear on your cat's skin, do not attempt to treat them yourself with ointments or shampoos, as similar-looking conditions may be due to a variety of sources, such as parasites (see page 38) or an allergic reaction. They may even be symptomatic of an internal disorder. Eczema, which shows as a raw-looking red inflammation of the skin, may be caused by too much fish in the diet or, in a neutered cat, a hormone imbalance. Your vet will advise you.

Stings

Cats often play with bees and wasps until they sustain their first sting. This usually teaches them to avoid buzzing insects in the future. A single sting is painful but not dangerous unless it is inside the cat's mouth or in the throat. Remove the sting if present and apply a cold water compress or ice pack if possible. If the swelling does not go down in a few hours or involves the throat, consult your veterinary surgeon.

Teeth and gums

Some cats are more prone than others to a build-up of tartar around the base of the teeth. If left unchecked, this can lead to gingivitis (a painful inflammation of the gums) and to the eventual loss of teeth. The warning signs are bad breath and difficulty in eating. Your vet will need to scrape off the tartar under a general anaesthetic, since it is extremely hard. Encouraging your cat to eat biscuity 'cat treats' and regularly brushing its teeth will help to prevent a build-up recurring.

▲ Even cats need to have their teeth cleaned to prevent tooth decay. You can buy special 'brushes' to make this process much easier.

Zoonoses

Zoonoses are diseases that are capable of spreading between animals and humans, but luckily there are very few of these. The most deadly zoonosis is rabies, which is controlled in the United Kingdom through the Pet Travel Scheme – ask your vet for details.

Toxoplasmosis is a very serious zoonosis, which is caused by a microscopic organism called *Toxoplasma*. This parasite can affect many animals, but only the cat spreads the infective cysts by voiding them in its faeces. An affected cat with the disease may show no symptoms at all, but the disease may cause congenital defects in a pregnant woman's unborn baby.

The normal way to prevent toxoplasmosis in the cat is to feed only heat-processed and well-cooked fresh meat, and to ensure that the cat does not catch or eat wild prey. You should always wash your hands after handling raw meat or fondling the cat; pregnant women should avoid changing cats' litter trays.

Ringworm is a fungus infection which may cause characteristic lesions on the skin. It is important that a cat with ringworm is taken for veterinary examination and is treated immediately, particularly because it is readily transmissible to humans. Do not allow a child any contact whatsoever with a cat showing symptoms of ringworm, as children are most at risk of cross-infection.

Parasites

▲ Fleas are disagreeable for both the cat and its owner. Your veterinary surgeon can advise on the best treatment. You can use a flea comb to remove fleas but it is not as effective as modern anti-flea medications.

Fleas

Even well-kept cats from very clean homes can pick up fleas from time to time. You can use either a flea spray or a spot-on product to treat the cat's coat, following the manufacturer's instructions. However, this treatment alone will not clear up a flea infestation. It will also be necessary to clean the cat's bedding, and to scrub its bed and all its haunts. The essential point is that fleas do not lay their eggs on the cat's fur but on its bedding and surroundings, and, unless these are cleaned thoroughly, the infestation will continue. You can use a spray manufactured to kill flea eggs on the bedding. It is advisable to treat a cat for fleas at the same time as it is wormed, because the two infestations may be linked.

▲ Cat flea

Lice

Cats may also be affected by lice, which are more difficult to see than fleas, although their white eggs, or nits, show up well, particularly on dark fur. Cats that constantly lick and bite themselves may be infested with lice and should be taken to a veterinary surgeon for examination. Your veterinary surgeon will be able to prescribe an effective spray which will need to be used for at least a month.

Worms

Both roundworms and tapeworms can affect cats. An infestation of roundworms may cause diarrhoea, loss of weight and poor condition. Sometimes these worms can be vomited. Tapeworms seldom cause any such symptoms, but segments of the worms can be seen around the anus of an infected cat.

▶ Tapeworms are quite common in cats and they appear as white 'rice grain' segments which stick to the hairs around the animal's rear end.

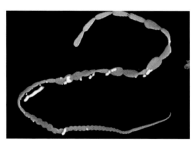

All kittens should be treated for roundworms as a matter of routine. The necessary wormers can be obtained from a chemist or from your veterinary surgeon. Administration is simple, but care must always be taken to give the correct dosage. Tapeworm

Life cycle of the tapeworm

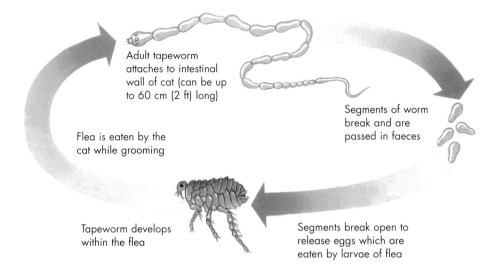

Adult tapeworm attaches to intestinal wall of cat (can be up to 60 cm (2 ft) long)

Flea is eaten by the cat while grooming

Segments of worm break and are passed in faeces

Tapeworm develops within the flea

Segments break open to release eggs which are eaten by larvae of flea

treatments are more difficult to administer, and if an infestation is suspected, then veterinary help must be sought without delay.

Ear mites

Ear mites can cause a great deal of suffering to cats and especially to kittens. Symptoms of ear trouble are scratching the ears, shaking or banging the head, and a brown encrustation within the ear canal. You should consult your veterinary surgeon without delay; he or she will be able to prescribe an effective treatment for the condition.

Mange mites

Cats can also be affected by a mite which causes skin canker with early symptoms of small bare patches on the ears and face. This can develop into a very serious skin condition unless it is treated promptly by a veterinary surgeon in the early stages.

Ticks

Cats are more likely to be found with ticks in some areas than in others. The ticks sink their head-parts into the cat's skin and engorge themselves by sucking the cat's blood. In a few days, when they are fully engorged, they drop off. It is not possible to remove a live tick completely with a pair of tweezers, as the head-part will remain firmly embedded. You should use a special tick-removing tool which can be bought from the pet shop or from your veterinary surgeon.

Administering medication

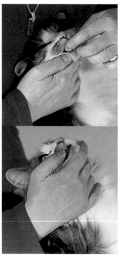

▲ To administer a tablet, hold the head back and ease it in to the mouth. Gently rub the throat until the cat swallows.

Administering medication

If a cat becomes nervous and needs to be restrained, it is best to wrap a towel around it. The best method of opening up a cat's mouth is to rest one hand on the top of its head and to press your thumb and forefinger against the angles of its jaws. First lower the cat's head and then raise it as this will create a small gap between the jaws at the front.

Administering tablets

A tablet held between the thumb and forefinger of your free hand can be inserted as shown, pushed well back on the tongue. Alternatively, use a pill applicator manufactured specially for animals.

Administering liquid medicine

If the mouth is opened as described, there will be sufficient space at the front of the jaws to allow liquid medicine to be trickled off a spoon, a few drops at a time. Lower the head to allow the cat to swallow, and repeat until the dose has been given. Alternatively, you can administer liquid medicine with a small plastic syringe.

Administering ear drops

Since ear trouble can occur among cats, a veterinary surgeon may have to prescribe ear drops at some time. Hold the cat's head to one side and insert the drops from their own applicator into the ear canal, gently massaging behind the ear in order to allow the drops to penetrate as far as possible. Gently clean away any discharge from the ear with great care.

Administering eye drops

When eye drops are prescribed, hold the cat's head back, and drop in the lotion from its own applicator to the inner corner of the eye. Continue to hold the head back for a moment or two to allow the drops to run over the whole eye surface.

◄ Administer liquids by holding back the cat's head and dropping or spooning them into its mouth.

First aid

If your cat is unfortunate enough to sustain a major injury, do call your veterinary surgery immediately to ensure that someone will be there. There are several things you can do while waiting for veterinary help.

● Make sure the cat is able to breathe without obstruction, which might necessitate the clearing of the airway. To do this, you should pull the tongue forward, gripping it gently with a piece of rough cloth or some towelling – a face flannel is ideal. Take care not to get bitten in the process.

● You can staunch any heavy bleeding by placing a clean folded handkerchief or tea towel over the cat's wound and then by applying enough pressure to stop the blood flow.

● Shock is countered by keeping the cat warm and quiet. Cover it with a blanket and apply a well-wrapped hot water bottle, or, alternatively, you can raise the temperature of the room overall.

● If the cat appears to have sustained a fracture, do not move it unless it is absolutely necessary to take it to the vet. Never try to apply any form of splint.

● If you suspect there are fractures, and the cat must be moved, it is best to slide it carefully on to a flat tray or board, which can be used as an effective temporary stretcher. If there are no fractures, you should lift the cat carefully into a secure carrier.

● If you have to give initial treatment to a wound yourself, bathe it with warm water, attempting to remove all superficial dirt. When the wound looks clean, bathe it again with saline solution made by dissolving one teaspoon of ordinary table salt in 600 ml (1 pint) of cooled boiled water. Do not use any disinfectant or antiseptic on the wound and leave it unbandaged until it has been professionally treated.

● If poisoning is suspected, then you must seek immediate veterinary advice, taking with you the packet or a sample of the poison you think has been taken. Treat as for shock.

● A small burn or scald can be cooled by immersion in cold water until help is at hand. Otherwise, wrap the animal in a clean tea towel, sheet or pillowslip to exclude the air, and seek immediate veterinary help.

Reproduction

Mating

Unfortunately, most matings between cats are unplanned. However, they are almost invariably successful. The female cat ovulates in response to a male and there are, therefore, always eggs ready to be fertilized.

Oestrus

Female cats are often capable of breeding from the age of about four months. In practice, they usually come into season in the first spring after the age of four months. They do not have a regular oestrous cycle, but come into season repeatedly throughout the year until they are mated. While they are on heat they adopt an unmistakable pattern of behaviour, which includes restless searching for a tom, and also calling toms to the house. The Foreign breeds, in particular, are very vocal at this time.

Pregnancy

Pregnancy in the cat lasts for approximately nine weeks, within the limits of 60 to 65 days. For the first five weeks of pregnancy, the queen will need no special attention, but her abdomen should not be handled carelessly. During the last month of pregnancy, when the kittens show, her appetite will increase markedly and she should be allowed as much good food as she will eat. In addition, a daily vitamin/mineral tablet will be a useful supplement.

Kittening

A pet cat should be allowed to have her kittens in the house. She will accept a box provided for her if it is a comfortable size, and placed in a dark corner where it will be warm and dry and easy for her to reach even when heavily pregnant. It should be lined thickly with newspapers which can be burned and replaced after the litter has been born.

It is unusual for a cat to need your help during the process of giving birth. She will clean the kittens herself, eat the placentas, and will then guide each kitten in turn to a teat for suckling.

The tom cat

The queen alone is responsible for the kittens, needing no help other than some praise from an understanding owner, and good food. Sometimes, when there are two queens in the household, one will help the other. The tom should not be allowed access to the kittens before they are four months old. While they are very young they are at risk, and kittens are quite frequently killed by the tom, especially when they are being raised in an outbuilding or shed and have no human protection.

Kittens' needs
Kittens open their eyes at between five and ten days and will continue to suckle from the queen to the age of seven to eight weeks. At three weeks of age, the litter starts to take an interest in their mother's food dish and the most precocious will try eating solids. The kittens can be tempted to try baby cereals, scrambled egg and some cooked, flaked white fish or cooked, minced chicken with the skin removed.

Surplus kittens
The queen will come into season again immediately after giving birth, which means that she could give birth to as many as three litters a year, with an average of six kittens to each litter. Kittens, especially mongrel ones, can be very difficult indeed to home, and if the whole litter cannot be kept or re-homed then the surplus kittens must be destroyed humanely. Drowning is a very cruel death, and it can never be recommended even for very young kittens. Instead, they should be taken to a veterinary surgeon, who will put them to sleep humanely.

▼ The grooming instinct is inborn in cats, and is seen in kittens as young as three weeks old.

Your questions answered

Our garden backs on to farmland and our three cats are always bringing in 'presents' of mice and voles. Short of moving, what can we do to stop them?

It is impossible to subdue your cats' natural hunting instincts. Unless your pets are confined to the house, which is not advised, they will continue to present you with trophies of their hunts. Town cats may not prey on rodents, but they are likely to bring home birds – sometimes quite large ones – or take to fishing in a neighbour's goldfish pond instead, so even moving is not a solution to the problem.

Constant scolding will not help either: a cat can be trained not to scratch the furniture or urinate indoors, but you will never persuade it to change its predatory nature. Young cats seem to be more active hunters and many grow out of it by the time they are three or four years old.

Is this true that cats can be a danger to new babies?

There have been reports of babies being smothered by cats which, presumably attracted by the warmth, have settled down to sleep on the cot pillow. These accidents are happily very rare, and could have been prevented by the simple expedient of fitting a special 'cat' net to the pram or over the cot when there are cats in the family. No small baby should ever be left alone with any pet, and strict standards of hygiene must be observed at all times.

My long-coated cat seems to swallow a lot of her fur when licking herself, which can make her sick. Is this harmful?

Long-coated cats often take in quantities of their own fur while grooming themselves and this can lead to the formation of hair balls when the hair compacts into a solid mass. This will cause digestive problems, as the hair ball is either vomited or causes a blockage in the intestines. As prevention is better than cure, be sure to groom your cat each day, removing all the loose hairs, then finish off by passing a slightly damp cloth over the cat's coat. Daily combing and brushing will also prevent the formation of dense mats of fur which have to be cut out.

We are shortly moving and I would like to know how best to settle my old cat into his new home.

The bustle and disruption of moving day would be bewildering to any cat, which may run off in fright to hide before the removal van has even arrived. To avoid frantic searches at the last minute, keep your cat indoors with a litter tray the night before, possibly in a room which has already been cleared, so that he need not be disturbed. He should travel not in the removal van but in a secure pet carrier (see pages 30 and 31) and, to begin with, be confined to one room in the new house, furnished with things with which he is familiar. Possessions are important to cats, so make sure you take with you your pet's bed, bedding and toys.

Keep your cat indoors for at least a week, providing a litter tray and gradually introducing him to more rooms. Eventually, take him into the garden prior to feeding time. Let him have a good sniff around and then bring him indoors for a favourite meal. After a few such excursions it will be safe to let your cat out alone, as he will have accepted the new house and garden, and will have learned his way around. The RSPCA also recommends that pets are microchipped so that if they stray they can be quickly reunited with their owners. Ask your vet for more details.

Can cats really see in the dark?

Although cats have very good eyesight and can adjust their pupils to see clearly in very dim conditions, they are unable to see in complete darkness.

I have heard that cats are fond of catnip. What is this and where can I get some?

Catnip is the dried leaves of the *Nepeta cataria*, or catmint, and some cats (not all) find the smell almost intoxicating. You can grow your own, or dried catnip can be bought in sachets from pet shops or by mail order and can be used in cushions and soft toys. Some cat toys and scratching posts are impregnated with catnip, and if your cat is one of those attracted by the smell, it acts as an attractive aid to training.

I recently saw a cat wearing a sort of plastic ruff. Was this just some unkind dressing up, or was there a reason for it?

What you saw was a veterinary device known as an Elizabethan collar. These are used to prevent cats from biting at wounds or from removing stitches from recent operations.

Life history

Scientific name	*Felis catus*
Gestation period	63 days (approx.)
Litter size	3–5 (average)
Birth weight	90 g (3 oz) – 140 g (5 oz)
Eyes open	10 days
Weaning age	42–56 days
Puberty	120–180 days
Adult weight	Males: 3.5 kg (8 lb) – 5.9 kg (13 lb) Females: 2.25 kg (5 lb) – 3 kg (7 lb)
Best age to breed	12+ months
Oestrus (or season)	Repeatedly in season January–October unless mated
Duration of oestrus	7–14 days
Retire from breeding	Males: 10 years Females: 8 years
Life expectancy	12–16 years

Index

Why not learn more about other popular pets with further titles from the bestselling RSPCA Pet Guide series?

PET GUIDE

0-00-718271-6

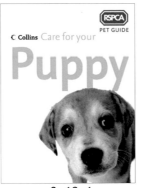

0-00-718268-6

0-00-718270-8

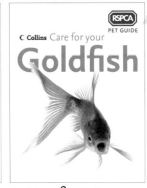

0-00-718272-4

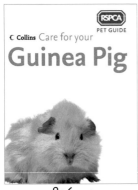

0-00-718269-4

0-00-719358-0

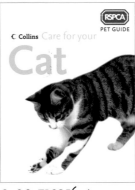

0-00-719356-4

Paperback
£4.99   48pp

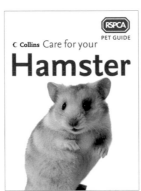

0-00-719357-2

0-00-719359-9

To order any of these titles, please telephone **0870 787 1732**
For further information about all Collins books, visit our website: **www.collins.co.uk**